Ancient India

Archaeology Unlocks the Secrets of India's Past

Ancient India

Archaeology Unlocks the Secrets of India's Past

By Anita Dalal

Monica L. Smith, Consultant

NATIONAL GEOGRAPHIC

Washington, DC

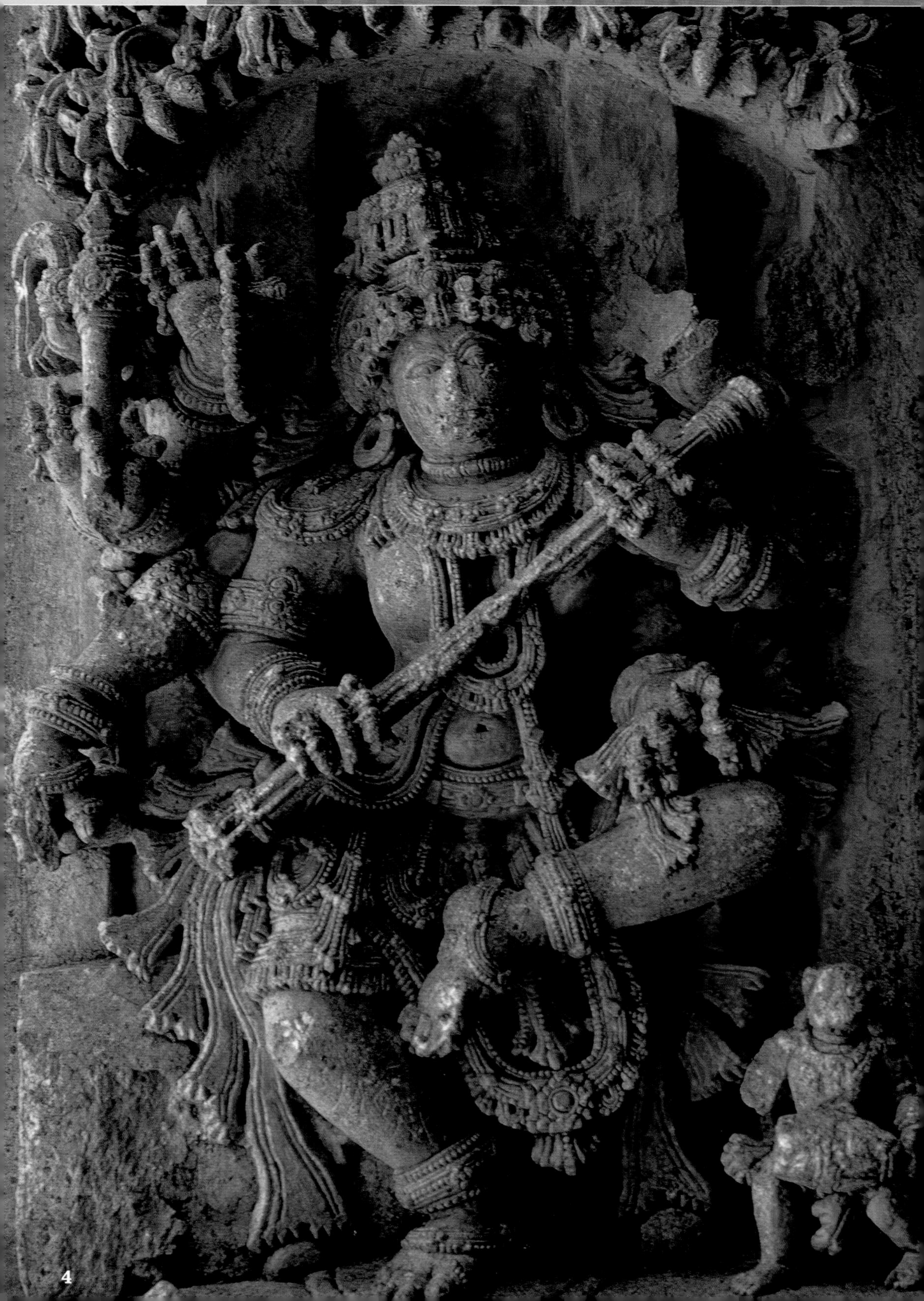

Contents

< This image from a temple in Somnathpur in southern India shows Saravasti, wife of the Hindu god Brahma, in an illustration from the ancient poem, the *Mahabarata*.

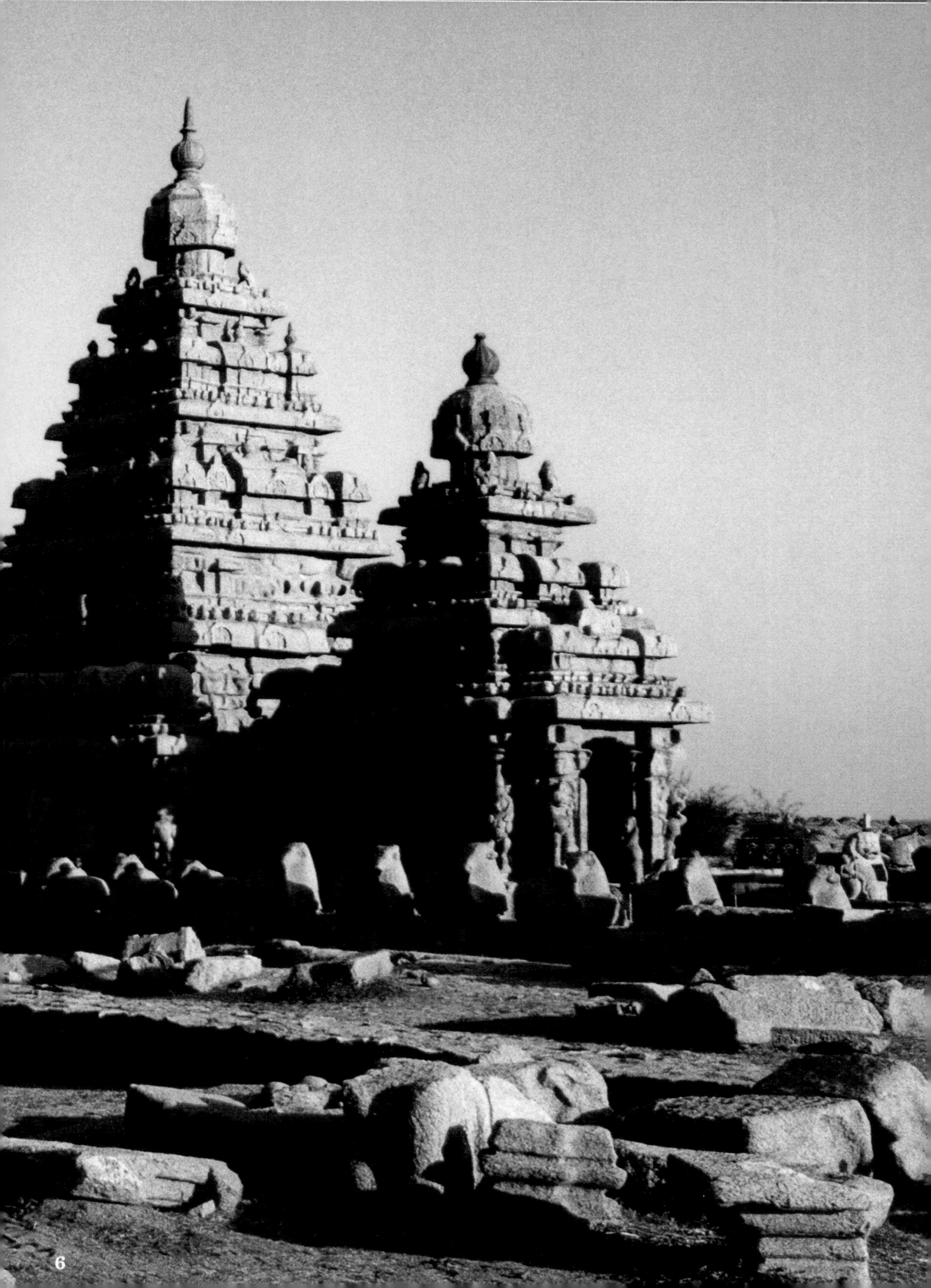

< Seventh-century A.D. Hindu temples at Mahabalipuram. Recent underwater explorations nearby have discovered the ruins of a city submerged beneath the ocean.

From the Consultant

Ancient India and modern India are both fascinating places for the archaeologist. Today, the Asian subcontinent is home to several nations, including Bangladesh, Pakistan, Sri Lanka, Nepal, and India. And in the past as well, there were many different cultures, languages, and religious traditions that were developed over many thousands of years. Some of the earliest civilizations in the world can be found here, with some of the first writing and the first cities. In ancient times, India was the home of two of the world's major religions, Hinduism and Buddhism; along with Islam, which was introduced later, they inspired some of the world's most famous architecture.

I have been fortunate to work in the Indian subcontinent for nearly twenty years on excavations, surveys, and mapping projects. I have found that people everywhere, from shopkeepers to government officials, are all interested in the past as a foundation for the present. Everywhere you go in India, you can see living heritage in the form of temples, tombs, and archaeological sites. There is also a profound respect for learning about the past. Archaeological news is often on the front page of the newspaper, and museums and archaeological sites are a favorite place for families to visit on their vacations.

Being able to work with scholars and students in India has been a wonderful experience both on a personal and on a scholarly level. The Indian subcontinent is increasingly visible today because of its vibrant economy and technological skills, and I encourage each of you to learn and read more about the archaeological heritage of this beautiful part of the world.

Monica L. Smith
Los Angeles, 2007

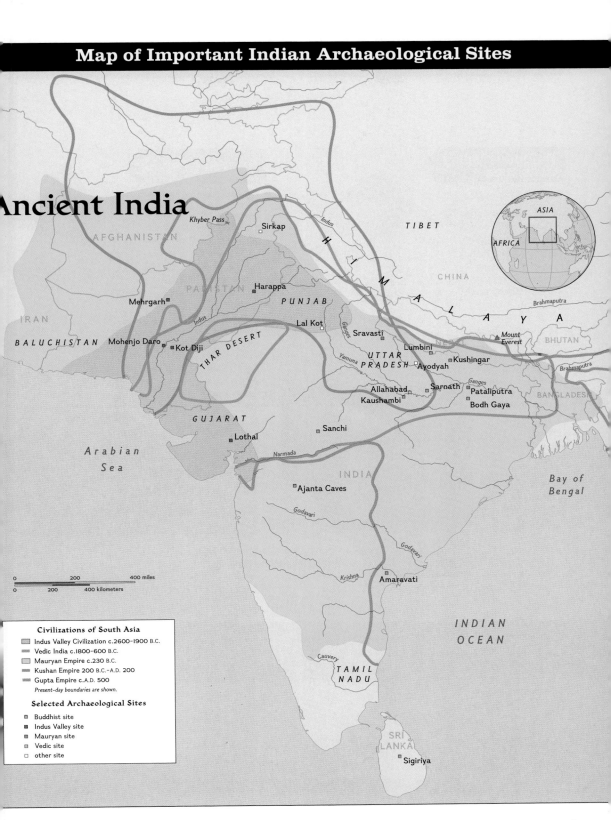

Ancient India

Khyber Pass

TIBET

ASIA

AFRICA

CHINA

Brahmaputra

Sirkap

Indus

H
I
M
A
L
A
Y
A

AFGHANISTAN

PAKISTAN

Harappa

Mehrgarh

PUNJAB

Lal Kot

Indus

Ganges

Sravasti

Mount
Everest

BHUTAN

NEPAL

IRAN

BALUCHISTAN

Mohenjo Daro

Kot Diji

THAR DESERT

Indus

Yamuna

UTTAR
PRADESH

Lumbini

Ayodyah

Kushingar

Sarnath

Pataliputra

Ganges

Brahmaputra

BANGLADESH

Allahabad

Kaushambi

Bodh Gaya

GUJARAT

Lothal

Sanchi

Narmada

INDIA

Arabian
Sea

Ajanta Caves

Bay of
Bengal

Godavari

Godavari

Krishna

Amaravati

INDIAN
OCEAN

Cauvery

TAMIL
NADU

SRI
LANKA

Sigiriya

| 0 | 200 | 400 miles |
| 0 | 200 | 400 kilometers |

Civilizations of South Asia
- Indus Valley Civilization c.2600-1900 B.C.
- Vedic India c.1800-600 B.C.
- Mauryan Empire c.230 B.C.
- Kushan Empire 200 B.C.–A.D. 200
- Gupta Empire c.A.D. 500

Present-day boundaries are shown.

Selected Archaeological Sites
- Buddhist site
- Indus Valley site
- Mauryan site
- Vedic site
- other site

The Indus Valley Civilization

ca 2600 B.C.–1900 B.C.

Beginning in about 7000 B.C., settlements emerged in northern India and what is now Pakistan. By the 3rd millennium, people were living in brick homes in large, planned cities such as Harappa and Mohenjodaro, with advanced plumbing systems. The people farmed and traded as far away as Mesopotamia, in what is now Iraq. They used a system of writing that has not yet been deciphered. The cities were abandoned around 1900 B.C., probably when rivers changed course and disrupted farming.

< A seal from Mohenjodaro with a figure and a form of writing at the top

The Vedic Period

ca 1800 B.C.–600 B.C.

After the abandonment of the great Indus Valley cities, farming peoples lived in smaller settlements in the Indus and Ganges Valleys. They merged with people who arrived from farther west in Asia. Storytellers created vedas, poems, and hymns that later became the basis of the Hindu religion. At the end of the period, this area was again a highly urban and wealthy state.

Timeline of Indian History

2000 B.C.

1000

0

◀ Indus Valley Civilization 2600–1900 B.C.

ca 1300 B.C.
The first parts of *Rigveda* are created

ca 6th–5th centuries B.C.
Buddha lives in northern India

326 B.C. Alexander the Great reaches South Asia

1st century B.C.
Kushans overthrow the Parthians

Vedic Period ca 1800–600 B.C.

Mauryan Empire ca 322–185 B.C.

The Mauryan Empire

ca 322–185 B.C.

The greatest of the Mauryan rulers, Ashoka, converted to Buddhism. The new faith, which had originated in the 6th to 5th centuries B.C., had become popular. Ashoka used its teachings to promote social welfare along India's extensive trade routes. He sent out missionaries that carried Buddhism to Sri Lanka, where it survived long after it declined in India itself.

The Gupta Empire

ca 320–497 A.D.

The Guptas were a Hindu dynasty who brought South Asia to a golden age of peace and profitable trade. Their achievements were echoed by outstanding sculpture and architecture, painting, and literature, and also by scientific achievement.
In the south, the Gupta dominance was echoed by that of the Vakataka dynasty at the same time.

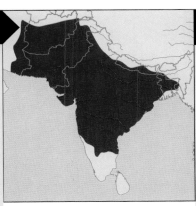

< A model of an ox cart from Harappa. It may have been used as a toy.

> A Gupta statue of Avalokiteshvara, a divine being who Buddhists believed would help them achieve Enlightenment.

ca 300 A.D.
Main period of temple building begins at Ajanta

477 A.D. Kasyapa I builds Sigiraya in Sri Lanka

1000

1206 A.D. The Delhi Sultanate brings northern India under Islamic rule

1498 A.D. Europeans arrive in India

1526 A.D. Mughal dynasty comes to power

1858 A.D. Start of formal British rule in India

2000 A.D.

1947 A.D. Creation of independent India and Pakistan

1971 A.D. Creation of Bangladesh

Gupta Empire
ca 320–497 A.D.

11

A Land of Stories

CHAPTER 1

How do we learn what we know about the past?

For generations, South Asian storytellers have entertained listeners with tales of gods and heroes. The adventures are as exciting as if they had just happened, but the stories are thousands of years old. They were passed on by word of mouth for centuries before they were written down. The stories are the basis of Indian religion and legends. They also hold clues about India's long past. South Asia was one of the first places where people started living together in cities, growing food, and using writing. Experts see these as key steps in the development of civilization.

< An actor is made up as the monkey god Hanuyaman for a play based on the *Ramayana*, one of India's most popular stories. Ancient tales are still part of everyday life for over a billion Indians.

The same step forward happened at about the same time in India, China, and Mesopotamia. Just why civilizations emerged at this particular time, no one knows.

Today, stories are not the only clues to India's past. There are also archaeological sites, sculptures, and artifacts such as seals that were used to print designs in soft clay. They mean little on their own. But for nearly 200 years experts have been trying to put ancient evidence together to understand India's past. Archaeologists are history's detectives. They take a few finds—some bricks, broken pottery, unknown writing—and try to create a picture of how a whole group of people once lived. The pictures change as new finds turn up.

The story of India that has emerged is remarkable. Not only was India a cradle of civilization, it was also the home of great religions. A series of ancient cultures had risen and fallen over many centuries.

What is India?

India has had its current shape only since 1947. It used to be much larger. When it is used to discuss the ancient world, "India" refers to the whole Asian subcontinent, a large peninsula bordered on two sides by ocean. Today the region is home to India, Pakistan, Nepal, Bangladesh, and the island of Sri Lanka in the Indian Ocean. These

< A storyteller and his monkey before a performance. The history passed on in old tales may be a clue to real events.

countries have political differences, particularly India and Pakistan. Both were created in 1947 by the split, or Partition, of the former India. Pakistan was originally split into two halves. The eastern part became Bangladesh in 1971. Since Partition, India and Pakistan have fought a series of wars.

An ancient past

In this book you will learn what archaeologists have discovered about the societies that lived in ancient India. During the

> Past and present: Modern Buddhist monks light candles during a festival at a seventh-century temple in Bodh Gaya.

V The physical evidence: This model of oxen pulling a cart was made nearly 4,500 years ago and shows us how goods were transported in ancient India.

< This stone relief from about the first century B.C. shows dancers following the rhythm of two drummers. Dance has always been popular in India, and it is depicted in many ancient temple sculptures.

18th and 19th centuries, the subcontinent was part of the British Empire. Much early archaeological work in India was done by British officials and military men who were interested in the region's past. In chapters 3 and 4, you will see how they found key clues to parts of history that had been forgotten. Some breakthroughs followed years of work, but others were accidental. In chapter 6, for example, you will see how a hunting expedition led not to tigers but to a far greater treasure.

Today's political divisions affect archaeology, even though the region shared a common past. Some Indian and Pakistani experts dispute findings

A Great Survey

The Archaeological Survey of India (ASI) was set up by the British government in the 19th century to record India's ancient sites. The ASI brought professional experts to India and coordinated their work. At times, the ASI was neglected by the government. In the 1930s one director even arrived to find wild monkeys had taken over his office. But the ASI has overseen most excavations in India for more than 150 years. You will see its work throughout this book. Since Indian independence in 1947, the ASI—like its equivalents in Bangladesh, Pakistan, and Sri Lanka—has been wholly staffed by local experts.

of years. But Afghanistan has been unsafe for archaeologists since 1978, when three decades of civil war, extremist governments, and foreign military invasion began. In chapter 5 you'll read the remarkable story of golden treasure found just weeks before fighting broke out there—treasure that everyone thought was lost forever.

that suggest that one country is superior to the other in any way. In chapter 7 you will learn how the study of the past in India has led to great controversy.

Outside influences

Modern politics sometimes makes it difficult to trace how influences arrived in India from other places. Afghanistan was the pathway into the subcontinent, through the Himalaya, for thousands

> Ancient Buddhist religious texts like these in a monastery in the Himalaya may still hold secrets about India's past.

CHAPTER 2

The Valley of the Indus

Who built India's first great cities?

Things sometimes look clearer from the air. That was what Michael Jansen decided when he became head of the German Research Project at Mohenjodaro in 1979. Instead of digging, as archaeologists often do, Jansen used another approach, which let him see more of the site. He mounted cameras on balloons to take bird's-eye photographs of brick ruins of what was once one of the largest urban sites in South Asia.

< Archaeologists don't always need a balloon to get into the air: American archaeologist Jonathan Mark Kenoyer uses ladders to photograph part of Harappa.

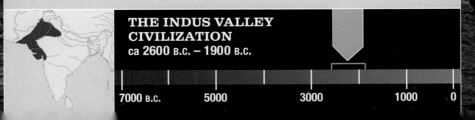

THE INDUS VALLEY CIVILIZATION
ca 2600 B.C. – 1900 B.C.

7000 B.C.   5000   3000   1000   0

Zooarchaeology

One way archaeologists try to understand such ancient peoples as those who lived at Mohenjodaro is through zooarchaeology—the study of animal bones. Bones turn up in many places on ancient sites, but especially in places where people threw their household garbage. We can tell from the size and shape of the bone whether an animal was wild or domesticated. By excavating layers of occupation, we can learn when people changed from being hunter-gatherers to living as farmers. We can also learn about the nearby natural environment from the kinds of amphibians, reptiles, or birds whose remains are found at a site.

Jansen's work confirmed what archaeologists already knew: About 4,500 years ago, Mohenjodaro was one of the world's largest cities—with some 35,000 citizens—and one of the cleanest. Its citizens were expert plumbers. Up to 700 wells brought underground water to the surface. Most homes had brick platforms used for bathing, and some even had bathrooms. Chutes carried used water into the streets, where brick-lined drains carried it away.

The water's fine

In the heart of the city stood a vast water tank 39 feet (11.8 m) long, 23 feet (7 m) wide, and 8 feet (2.4 m) deep. The

▽ So much care was taken in building the Great Bath in Mohenjodaro that experts believe that water must have had a religious meaning for the people.

walls of the tank, or Great Bath, were made of close-fitting bricks waterproofed with a layer of tar, called bitumen. The pool was surrounded by a complex of

walls and passages, so it may have been part of a group of buildings.

It seemed that the people at Mohenjodaro placed great importance on water. They may have used it in religious rituals. Cleansing with water is still an important part of religion in India today. The plumbing and sewers of Mohenjodaro were remarkable. When they were built around 2600 B.C., the city was one of the most advanced in the world. It was a busy center for about a thousand years.

The mound of the dead

Mohenjodaro was discovered in the 1920s by R. D. Banerji of the ASI. Banerji came across the site while he was exploring the lower valley of the Indus River (now in Pakistan), which is today a dry and barren region. The name Mohenjodaro—"mound of the

△ Water still plays a key role in Indian religions. Here Hindu pilgrims bathe in a waterfall near the source of the holy Narmada River.

dead" in the local Sindhi language— referred to a dome-shaped Buddhist monument, called a stupa. But beneath and around the stupa, Banerji could see the brick remains of a large, much older, city.

Banerji dug some pits down into the ruins. The layers of remains showed that the city had been occupied in four different stages. In the most recent stage, near the surface, he found coins from the third century A.D. This meant that the bottom layers were much older. At the lowest level, Banerji was excited to find three small squares of soft stone carved with images and lettering. He recognized them as seals. People once pressed the seals into soft clay as a mark to identify themselves, just as we might use a signature today.

Clues from the seals

Someone else would also be excited about the seals. Banerji's colleague at the ASI, Sir John Marshall, was digging at a site named Harappa some 350 miles (565 km) north in the Indus Valley. He had not found much. But Banerji remembered that a dig there in the 1870s had found a single square seal. It had been carved with an image of a bull and some strange lettering. It seemed to Banerji that the seals might link the two cities in time.

John Marshall agreed that the seals had been created by the same

▼ Mohenjodaro has been explored for over 90 years—but the ruins cover a huge area, and there may be more secrets to discover.

Reading the Signs

In the late 20th century, scholars began to decode the marks on the Harappa and Mohenjodaro seals. They identified more than 400 different signs. That was too many for an alphabet, where letters are combined to make words. But it was too few for a language in which each word has a pictogram, or sign. That takes thousands of signs. The experts guessed that the writing on the seals combined letters and pictograms. They also figured that it gave the name and occupation of the owner of the seal. Scholars do not agree how the script might be related to modern languages.

The experts worked out that the pictograms might group people into clans. They often showed animals or heavenly bodies, so perhaps there was an elephant clan or a moon clan. The "letter" symbols likely were the name of the individual.

< Archaeologist Jonathan Mark Kenoyer (left) examines pottery made by local craft workers at Harappa that imitates ancient styles.

people. But the writing looked so different from local Sanskrit that he wondered whether those people were from India at all. Perhaps the seals were clues to the existence of a civilization that had been forgotten.

Perfect penpals

Marshall solved the mystery in a way that was common at the time. He sent drawings of the seals to a magazine, the *Illustrated London News*, which published them. His request for information soon paid off. One scholar contacted him to say that the seals were of a type common in ancient Mesopotamia, in what is now Iraq. Then another wrote to say that he had actually found just such a seal buried beneath a temple in a Mesopotamian kingdom named Kish.

∧ Seals from Indus Valley sites feature animals such as bulls, along with markings that are not yet understood but may be proper names.

That find dated from 2300 B.C.

Marshall goes to work

Not only did Marshall now have a date for his cities, he also had possible evidence that the people who lived in the Indus River Valley had traded across Asia with the Mesopotamians. He knew little else about them, so he

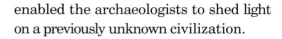

ordered extensive excavations at both Harappa and Mohenjodaro.

Harappa had been badly damaged over the years. Millions of bricks had been removed by laborers to build a railroad. But Mohenjodaro was in better condition. Work there was on a vast scale—six archaeologists and 800 laborers worked for six years. The massive effort provided a lot of information about the sites, which enabled the archaeologists to shed light on a previously unknown civilization.

Digging the cities

The 1920s excavations showed that Mohenjodaro and Harappa were similar—and highly sophisticated. The people lived in brick houses at least two stories high that surrounded courtyards. Mohenjodaro seemed to be arranged in zones. The city had a raised area that might have been a defensive citadel, although it did not seem to have fortified walls.

Near the water tank at the center of the city was another large structure that the original diggers linked with food storage. They named it the Granary. Later archaeologists say that there is no evidence that it was used to store grain. They call it the Great Hall. The same kinds of pottery and jewelry were found in both cities, showing that the people made similar crafts.

A widespread culture

The peoples of the cities were given the name Harappans, after the first city to be discovered. As the 20th century went on, archaeologists found more than a thousand Harappan sites. Harappan influence had spread throughout the Indus Valley and much of South Asia and

< Experts think that stone figures like this must have had a religious meaning because they were so carefully made. This small figure may show a priest.

around the northern coast of the Arabian Sea. Covering 250,000 square miles (648,000 sq km), the Indus Valley civilization was the most extensive of all ancient civilizations.

Clues from the west

More evidence about the Harappans came from Mesopotamia. The people there referred to the Indus region as Meluhha. A seal found in Mesopotamia describes a person as "the translator of the Meluhhan language." Experts believe that this probably means that some of the traders who went back and forth between the two civilizations were bilingual.

Oh my, Oman

Evidence kept appearing of the links between the Harappans and cultures far to the west. At Lothal in India, archaeologists in the 1950s found evidence of trade across the Persian Gulf, on the other side of the Arabian Sea. There, at Dilmun in Oman, excavators found seals and sets of traders' weights identical to those found in India.

Lothal had been a busy, noisy place. Indian archaeologist S. R. Rao found workshops with signs of bead-making and metal-working. Experts reason that materials such as precious stones or shells were gathered across a wide area. They were then brought to

∨ This painting reconstructs a Harappan house based on archaeological evidence. The flat roof is used for preparing food. Downstairs, a servant helps his master wash. The dirty water runs out from the house into a drain in the street.

centers like Lothal to be made into goods for sale or export.

Back in time

A discovery in 1955 by the Pakistan Department of Archaeology finally made the roots of the Indus Valley civilization clearer. At Kot Diji, about 25 miles (40 km) from Mohenjodaro, Fazal Ahmed Khan dug through three layers of Harappan culture. The fourth layer dated from 2950 B.C., before Harappa had become a major city. Khan found pottery there that used designs familiar from later pottery. The town itself was laid out in Harappan style, with neat streets of brick homes inside a stone wall.

Kot Diji and other sites showed that the Harappan culture was the result of a long period of local development. Other discoveries enabled archaeologists to go even

further back in time to learn about the very beginnings of settled life.

A remarkable site

In 1974 French and Pakistani teams began digging at Mehrgarh, in the dry, hilly region of Baluchistan (in what is now Pakistan). A river had changed course and created a cliff that exposed layers of remains. They found a series of settlements that had been abandoned and rebuilt, a little farther south each time. Experts used a technique called radiocarbon dating to find out how old the site was.

All living things contain the chemical carbon. When they die, the carbon begins to decay at a steady rate. Measuring how much carbon has decayed reveals the age of the original object. Charcoal from the lowest layer at Mehrgarh came from around 7000 B.C.

Work at Mehrgarh is still going on, over 30 years since it began. It is unusual for

> This clay model of a boat was discovered at Lothal, which was a center for shipping. The town may have had the earliest harbor in the world.

> These stone weights from Lothal were used in trade across the Indian Ocean—identical weights have been found in ancient Mesopotamia.

archaeologists to be able to work on the same site for so long. It is also unusual to be able to uncover so many layers of occupation. That makes Mehrgarh a remarkable site in the story of ancient India.

In the 1980s, studies of bones showed that, in about 6000 B.C., the inhabitants of Mehrgarh had switched from hunting to raising sheep, goats, and cattle. They grew crops, too. Some buildings had small compartments for storing wheat and barley. The shapes of the grains could still be seen, pressed into the mud bricks. By the late 4000s B.C., the citizens of Mehrgarh were living in two-story homes and making pots on wheels.

The end of the Harappans

Mehrgarh showed how the cultures of the Indus Valley grew. From such villages, great cities arose as the Harappans expanded throughout the Indus Valley.

For several hundred years, those cities grew and traded over a large area. But by 1900 B.C. they faced problems that can still be seen in cities today, such as overcrowding and shortages of food and water. Then a crisis hit the cities in the shape of an earthquake or some other geological activity that made some of the rivers dry up. Archaeologists have found many Harappan sites that are now in areas of desert, and satellite images show that ancient river courses shifted dramatically. When the rivers shifted, many people who lived near them may have moved to cities that were not affected. But their arrival may have doomed the very cities that took them in.

After the Harappans

CHAPTER 3

Who took the place of the Harappans?

In 1981 archaeologist S. R. Rao began exploring a ruined city on the seabed off the coast of Gujarat. Rao, an adviser to the Marine Archaeology Unit of India's National Institute of Oceanography, used four divers with scuba gear to survey the site, which stretched more than half a mile (0.8 km) from the coast. About 3,500 years ago, the city had stood beside a river. Then it was submerged as the coast was worn away. Rao's team found strong defensive walls—and many interesting

< The carvings on a 13th-century Hindu temple at Somnathpur illustrate scenes from the *Mahabarata*, a long poem created in the Vedic period.

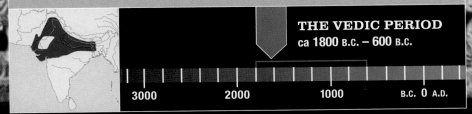

THE VEDIC PERIOD
ca 1800 B.C. – 600 B.C.

3000   2000   1000   B.C. 0 A.D.

29

artifacts. These included a seal carved with the image of a three-headed animal, pottery with inscriptions in the writing of the Indus Valley civilization, and triangular anchors made of iron.

The discovery was thrilling for two reasons. First, it showed that cities still existed in India soon after the fall of the Indus Valley culture. Scholars had once believed that no real cities had existed until much later, about 600 B.C. Instead, it seemed that the descendants of the Harappans had lived not only in small villages but also in larger settlements.

▽ A Hindu reads the *Ramayana* in Sanskrit. Many styles of writing may be used to write Sanskrit: This script is called Devanagari. It has been used in India since the 12th century.

The second reason for excitement was that both the seal and the triangular anchors had been mentioned in the *Mahabarata*, one of India's ancient epic poems. Although the poem was first written down in about the 6th or 5th century B.C., it may already have been hundreds of years old by then. It describes a city named Dwarka, which had once been ruled by Sri Krishna, who later became a Hindu god. The city had been submerged in a great flood.

No one knew whether the lost city was real or not, although some experts had begun searching for it in the 1930s. Now Rao anounced that he had found it—and that archaeology had shown the *Mahabarata* to be historically accurate.

A language mystery

Many archaeologists would not go as far as Rao. The ties between the underwater site and the poem might be a coincidence. But experts had long thought that the ancient poems and hymns of India might contain some clues about the past.

Much of the early work in understanding the people who created these works was done in the 18th century by an unusual detective named William Jones. Jones was a British judge who was sent to work in the province of Bengal in the 1780s. Jones loved India; he helped start the

△ A Hindu scholar studies one of the Vedas, the basis of the Hindu faith; the Vedic period in India is sometimes called the Indo-Aryan period.

You Sound Like a Fossil!

When William Jones realized that Sanskrit was related to ancient Greek and Latin, it was not just a breakthrough in the study of India's history. It was also the start of a new kind of archaeology, called linguistic paleontology. Paleontology is the study of fossils. Jones's approach was like studying the "fossils" of language—the parts of modern languages that began in much earlier languages. Linguists look for aspects—such as specific words or the order of words in a sentence—that are similar in different languages. That helps them group languages that share a common origin, which are said to belong to a family. The Indo-European family includes English, Russian, and Italian, as well as many languages of India and Iran, such as Farsi, Hindi, and Bengali. Dozens of languages came from the same root.

Asiatic Society of Bengal to coordinate study of its history and monuments. He also set out to learn Sanskrit, the holy language of India's ancient religion, Hinduism.

In the 1790s, Jones made a startling claim. He had noticed that many Sanskrit words resembled similar words in ancient Greek and Latin. The grammar of the languages also seemed similar.

∧ Many Indian farmers still follow a lifestyle that would have been familiar to ancient people, using cattle or bullocks to pull carts. India has more cattle than any other country: about 200 million head.

Sanskrit was clearly related to the languages of Western Asia and Europe, showing that the subcontinent had been in contact with other regions over a long period. The languages likely originated in areas of West Asia where farming first began. Experts know that domesticated plants and animals spread out from West Asia. People may have migrated in a similar way, bringing their languages with them. Later experts named the family of languages Indo-European.

The written record

The ancient ritual songs and poems of India are invaluable to historians. They are some of the oldest written works from anywhere in the world that can still easily be read today. There are four Vedas, or books of hymns, and two long poems, named the *Ramayana* and the *Mahabarata*. The oldest work is the *Rigveda*, whose earliest parts may date to around 1300 B.C. The Vedic poems contain the roots of Indian civilization as we know it today, but some of the themes are surprising. Alongside descriptions of cattle raising, the hymns and poems also contain details of warfare and raids. There is little physical evidence that the Vedic period was particularly violent, however.

The Vedas and poems describe a number of destructive gods. They also describe how people settled on the river plains, herding livestock and growing grain. We know from the stories that people used copper and bronze weapons, had horses, and held their chiefs in high regard. Feasting was an important part of their social life.

A pottery key

In the 1950s, B. B. Lal of the ASI used the *Mahabarata* to locate more than 30 ancient sites, where he found copper tools and horse bones associated with the Vedic way of life. Another clue about patterns of culture was found in a simple type of artifact: pottery.

Painted Gray Ware turned up all over the northern region of Punjab—now divided between India and Pakistan—and central northern India. Experts concluded that the decorated pottery must have been made by the descendants of the Harappans. It seemed that, although the great cities had disappeared, the culture itself survived. Smaller settlements spread across northern India as people learned new ways of farming. In the Ganges Valley, meanwhile, hunter-gatherers were also influenced by these changes. They began to farm and settle in villages.

▽ This 17th-century painting of a scene from the *Ramayana* shows the monkey hero Hanuyaman meeting Rama's wife, Sita. Hanuyaman is portrayed as a great general—but there is little physical evidence that warfare was particularly important in ancient India.

In a God's Footsteps

Where did the Buddha walk in India?

O n his first big dig, Indian archaeologist S. N. Chowdhary faced a huge challenge. He had only a month to get results before the site was destroyed by builders working on a nearby dam. Chowdhary was studying for an advanced degree when he found a mound of bricks about 40 feet (12 m) high in a remote part of Gujarat in 1957. He guessed the domed structure was a stupa, a monument that often stood above the remains of devout Buddhists.

< **This 40-foot-high (12 m) golden statue of Buddha was created in the 17th century in a monastery at Ladakh high in the Himalaya in northern India.**

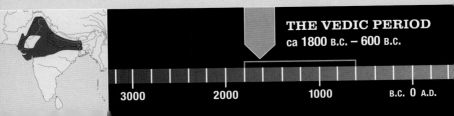

THE VEDIC PERIOD
ca 1800 B.C. – 600 B.C.

3000   2000   1000   B.C. 0 A.D.

The dam builders wanted to use the mound as a source of brick. The authorities did not want to hold up the work. Chowdhary's supervisor gave him a month to prove that he was right. Otherwise the dam would go ahead—and Chowdhary would be thrown out of school.

The young man started digging—fast. He got lucky. Within days, he found a statue of the Buddha. He had made his point—and saved the stupa.

A remarkable find

It took three years of slower work to reach the heart of the stupa, which held a small round stone casket. A Sanskrit inscription on the vessel recorded that the stupa had been built in the middle of the fourth century a.d. But it also made a more astonishing claim: "This is the abode of the relics of Dashabala." Dashabala

▽ A carving from the stupa at Sanchi shows a scene from the Buddha's life in which Prince Siddhartha rides in a chariot before giving up his throne to become a religious leader.

was an alternate name for the founder of Buddhism. The golden globe inside the casket—now kept at Baroda University—may hold the ashes of the Buddha himself. We will never know for sure.

Buddha or "the Enlightened One" was a name given to Siddhartha Gautama, a sixth-century B.C. Indian prince. He preached that people could achieve a state called Nirvana, which was free of desire or suffering. Unlike Vedic religions, Buddhism did not rely on priests to instruct worshipers. Buddhists could meditate to achieve Nirvana. Buddha's followers later spread his teachings through East and Southeast Asia. Today, Buddhism has over 350 million followers.

But little over a century before Chowhdary's find, Buddhism had been forgotten in India. It only became clear in the early 19th century that Buddha had been an Indian.

▽ **The gateway to the stupa at Sanchi was carved in the 1st century B.C. with scenes from the life of Buddha.**

Bringing it all together

Although Buddhism had disappeared in India, on its borders the faith was still practiced on the island of Sri Lanka and in the mountains of Nepal and Tibet. Monastery libraries held ancient stories of the Buddha's life. In the thousand or so years that the faith dominated India, the region had been a popular destination for travelers, who described it in ancient Greek, Latin, and Chinese records.

The man who brought the literary sources together with the physical ruins was Alexander Cunningham, a British army engineer. Cunningham began exploring Buddhist monuments in 1834, when he dug into a stupa at

Sarnath. Then he got hold of a French translation of a work by a Chinese Buddhist named Hsuan Tsang, who had visited India in the seventh century, more than a thousand years after Buddha had lived. Buddhism was in decline, he wrote, but still popular.

Buddha's life

Cunningham used the pilgrim's account as a guidebook to carry out what he thought would be a brief survey of ancient remains. In the end, he spent twenty-five years on his quest and did not finish until he was well into his seventies.

Often he worked quickly, recording what he could before hurrying on. There was so much to do. Northern India was home to many sites linked to Buddha. The four most important were Lumbini in Nepal, said to be Siddartha's birthplace; Bodh Gaya in the state of Bihar, where he meditated beneath a banyan tree; Sarnath, where the Buddha preached his first sermon; and Kusinara, where he died.

But Cunningham also visited sites that revealed the world in which Buddhism had thrived. At Kaushambi, a village of only 2,000 people, he found earthen ramparts that marked the walls of a huge ancient city 4 miles (6.4 km) around.

< This early statue of Buddha shows him in one of his traditional poses, with one hand raised in blessing to his followers.

An urban world

Later archaeologists explored the same sites up to a century after Cunningham. They discovered a series of ruined settlements that showed that the rise of Buddhism had coincided with a burst of city-building in the Ganges Valley, east of the ancient centers of the Indus Valley.

The archaeologists tracing this change had an invaluable aid. The urban citizens used a kind of pottery that was dark but highly polished. This Northern Black Polished Ware, or NBP Ware, is like a fingerprint for identifying sites: It was so well made that it has a glistening surface, almost like silver. It turned up in the lower

⋀ Pilgrims set up colorful prayer flags to decorate this tree in a sacred garden in Lumbini, which they believe is Buddha's birthplace.

levels of many cities, showing that they had all been founded at about the same time. The population must have grown, and with it trade and wealth.

The new merchants and traders wanted a new faith, and many found it in Buddhism. Stupas built in the cities and countryside show that the new faith had an enthusiastic welcome. Disciples used their money to build monuments to proclaim their devotion. Monasteries were founded along trade routes. They provided a way for religion and trade to develop together.

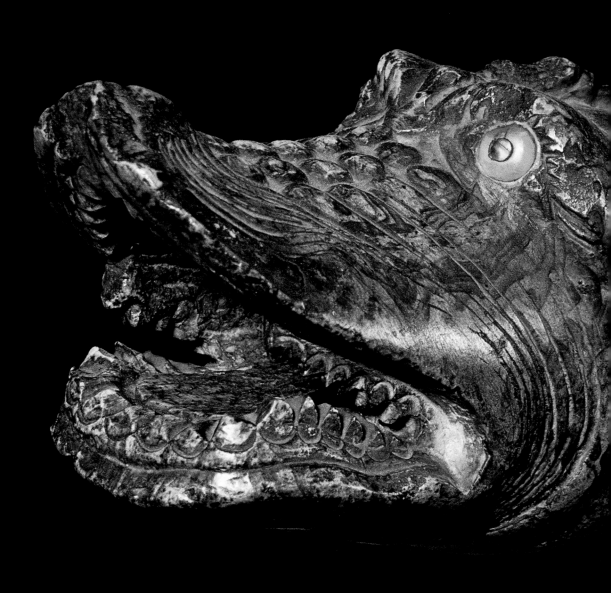

A Changing World

What did the ancient pillars mean?

After India achieved independence from Britain in 1947, the politicians who had led the independence campaign looked to the future. But they did not forget the past. The new government created a flag for the new country. In 1950 they added a crest to that flag. The crest was a wheel, or chakra, which was a symbol of order and balance. The chakra symbol was over 2,000 years old. It had been discovered on the base of a carving showing four seated lions,

⟨ This makara was carved in India in the 2nd century B.C. during the Mauryan period. The makara is a crocodile-like creature from Hindu mythology.

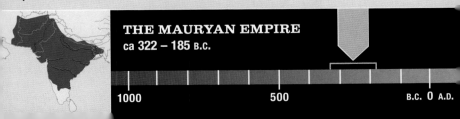

THE MAURYAN EMPIRE
ca 322 – 185 B.C.

1000   500   B.C. 0 A.D.

▲ One of King Ashoka's pillars looks over a ruined stupa at Sravasti. Legend says that the king built 84,000 stupas to show his devotion to the Buddha.

facing in four different directions.

The carved lions became another symbol of the country. They appear on Indian banknotes—even though there are few lions left in modern India.

Pillars of wisdom

The lions and the chakra came from the top of a tall pillar at Sarnath in northern India. Similar pillars had been found between the 1600s and the 1800s. They were all carved with inscriptions—but no one could read them until 1837.

A British official in India, James Prinsep, saw copies of inscriptions from the stone railings surrounding the Buddhist stupa at Sanchi. They were short lines in the same script that was on the pillars. Each line ended in the same characters. Prinsep guessed that the inscriptions listed people who had paid to build the stupa. In that case, the word repeated in each inscription might be "given," or "danam" in Sanskrit.

It was the key Prinsep needed. He worked out the

◄ The lions from Ashoka's column are a symbol of India. The spoked wheel, or chakra, beneath them appears on the national flag.

characters for *d, n,* and *m,* and went on to break the code. The messages on the pillars were a set of rules for living a good life, a little like the teachings of Buddhism. They were the work of a king who called himself Piyadassi.

Prinsep learned that another name for Piyadassi was Ashoka. Ashoka was one of the Mauryan kings who ruled much of India in the 300s and 200s B.C. In a few dozen inscriptions, Ashoka recorded not only the way he wanted his subjects to live, but also the history of his own reign.

Ashoka boasted that he had built roads to encourage trade. Ashoka was a Buddhist. He built many stupas in India and trained monks to carry the faith overseas. It was thanks to his efforts that the faith spread into Sri Lanka.

Western ideas

Experts working at the Great Stupa of Amaravati have found thousands of coins buried during the building of the stupa from the third century B.C. to the second century A.D. But some of the coins had writing in ancient Greek—and images that looked just like Greek statues.

The coins were the work of the Bactrians. They had arisen in what is now Afghanistan in the second century B.C. and expanded their domain into what is now Pakistan. Their culture was heavily influenced by the ancient Greeks. In 326 B.C., Alexander the Great had led his Greek armies as far east as the Indus River as he created

∨ **The Parthian city of Sirkap was laid out along Greek lines, with a grid of streets and temples supported by Greek columns.**

an empire that stretched from Egypt across Central Asia.

Soon Alexander headed back west—his troops were tired of constant fighting and wanted to go home. But he left settlers who brought Greek and Persian (Iranian) influences to Pakistan and Afghanistan. The Bactrians and their successors, the Parthians, also incorporated Greek influence. They built cities such as Sirkap, in Pakistan, that were modeled on western examples.

In the 1st century B.C., the Parthians were conquered by another dynasty from Central Asia, the Kushans. The Kushans built an empire where artists produced work that reflected influences from as far away as Rome, Italy.

Archaeology and War

War is terrible for anyone who gets caught up in it—including archaeologists. Sites are often quite remote, and people working there cannot be protected. Experts studying the Bactrians, for example, could not work in Afghanistan for over two decades. A civil war was followed by a Soviet military occupation. Then more fighting brought the anti-Western Taliban to power. And finally the U.S.-led invasion in 2001 sparked more fighting. In such cases, archaeologists have little choice: They have to leave for their own safety and hope that the valuable sites are not damaged in the violence.

The Bactrian gold

In 1978 Victor Sariandi, an archaeologist from Uzbekistan, found remarkable evidence of Bactria. He was working in northern Afghanistan at a site named Tillya Tepe, or "golden hill," but was at the point of giving up. The weather had turned wet and cold. Worse, a civil war had broken out in the country. One morning armed horsemen visited the site and threatened the archaeologists before riding off.

< This piece of carved ivory once decorated a chair that was made under the Kushans in the 1st century A.D.

Then a workman made a startling discovery. He uncovered the remains of a tomb with a wooden coffin holding a skeleton surrounded by precious artifacts. While Sariandi was exploring the tomb, news came that another had been found. And another, and another. There were seven in all.

∧ This clasp made from gold inlaid with pale green turquoise held together the clothes of a Bactrian noble.

For the last tomb, Sariandi had only a week before the site closed for winter. He did as much as he could, and then took what he had found—more than 20,000 objects—to the museum in the capital, Kabul. The so-called Bactrian gold gave a unique insight into Bactria in about 100 A.D. The finds included objects with Indian influences, such as carvings of hump-backed oxes, but also others that had Roman, Persian, and Greek influence.

> The Bactrian Aphrodite is a Roman goddess, but she has a forehead mark like Indian deities.

Meeting point

Bactria had been an important meeting place on the so-called Silk Road, the most important trade route in Asia. The "road" was not like the superhighways we are familiar with today, but a network of pathways that connected China in the east with the Mediterranean in the west. Traders carried goods along the Silk Road—and they also carried ideas and beliefs. The Bactrian gold was spectacular evidence of how different influences had come together.

But the fate of the gold was uncertain. Sariandi had to leave it at the museum. It was time for him to get out of the country. Afghanistan was growing too dangerous to stay. In 1979, troops from the Soviet Union invaded Afghanistan. That sparked more violence and began a series of bitter wars that is still going on. It remained too dangerous for Sariandi to go back to Tillya Tepe—or even to Kabul. As for the Bactrian gold itself, it was rumored to have been lost in the war-torn decades following the Soviet invasion.

The Age of the Guptas

Who painted the caves of Ajanta?

About two hundred years ago, bored British cavalry officers on duty in the countryside in central India paid a young man to show them where they could go hunting. He led them to a gorge where steep cliffs rose up above a U-bend in the Waghora River. It looked like good tiger country. The men got their guns ready and were climbing down into the gorge when one of them got a huge surprise. Staring from

< This massive statue of a reclining Buddha was carved from the solid rock in Cave 26 at Ajanta.

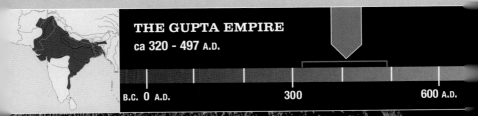

THE GUPTA EMPIRE
ca 320 - 497 A.D.

B.C. 0 A.D.   300   600 A.D.

∧ The 70-foot-deep (20 m) ravine at Ajanta was used by hundreds of Buddhist monks as a retreat where they could pray and think about their faith.

the face of the cliffs was a huge face— a giant carving of the Buddha. As they got closer, the men saw that a carved doorway near the statue led into the cliff. What lay inside? The men lit flaming torches and began to explore.

Forgotten treasures

The hunters had stumbled upon what is now one of the world's most famous archaeological sites: the caves of Ajanta. Twenty-nine caves had been carved into the rock of the cliff. Four were places for Buddhists to worship. The rest of the caves were monasteries: An underground courtyard was surrounded by small rooms where monks and nuns could sleep. They were decorated with more carved images of the Buddha. Colorful murals covered almost every wall. The caves were well preserved: They had been almost forgotten for over a thousand years. Wild animals had been the only regular visitors.

A king's boasts

Such a vast work of art was not created overnight. Experts dated the oldest caves to the second century B.C., and the last to 700 years later. Much of the work had been done after A.D. 300, at a time of great artistic achievement in India.

During the first half of the 1800s, clues to this golden age emerged from inscriptions on coins. They recorded the deeds of an emperor named Samudragupta. At Allahabad, a stone

Spreading the Word

It took many years for the rest of the world to hear about the Ajanta caves. At the time they were discovered, the only way for people to learn of new discoveries was either to visit them or to read about them in newspapers and magazines. The articles were often illustrated with engravings based on the work of amateur artists. In the 1840s a British artist made copies of the largest paintings at Ajanta and sent them to London—but they were burned in a fire. The same fate destroyed copies made in the 1870s.

In the 1920s, the first photographs were taken of the murals. When the pictures reached Europe, they caused a sensation.

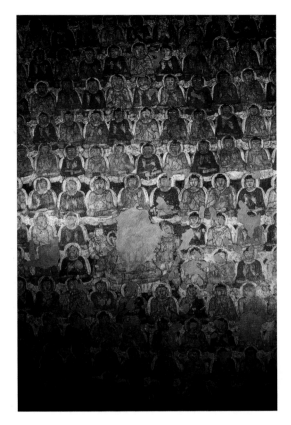

> This mural illustrates the "miracle at Saravasti," when Buddha filled the sky with images of himself.

∨ The monastery caves had an underground courtyard and rooms where monks and nuns slept.

pillar originally erected by Ashoka in the fourth century B.C. had been altered to celebrate the same king. It told how he had conquered other lands and boasted that he cared for the poor and was a skilled poet.

Such records are not always reliable: Kings might exaggerate their importance and achievements. But information on Samudragupta came from another source. French experts had translated the travel accounts of the Chinese monk Fa Hsien, who had spent about ten years in India in the

Gaps in the Record

It has been hard for experts to learn some details about the Guptas. Many Gupta sites continued to be occupied later, which covered up the Gupta remains. The problem is not unique to India. In many places archaeologists come up against periods from which they can find few objects or ruins, even though they might have evidence from an earlier age. The reasons for these gaps in the record vary. Evidence might have been destroyed in war or invasion. Or there might have been a natural disaster, such as a flood or an earthquake. Or it might be a matter of luck: The evidence is out there, but no one has found it yet.

fifth century. He described a peaceful and wealthy country where agriculture was highly successful and merchants sold goods from as far away as the Mediterranean Sea.

The mighty Guptas

The emperor who ruled over this golden age was Samudragupta's son, Chandragupta II. Father and son were two of the outstanding rulers of the Guptas. The dynasty ruled much of northern India from A.D. 320 to 497, although their influence spread farther and lasted longer. In fact, the major caves at Ajanta were created by a dynasty named the Vakataka, who dominated southern India near the end of the Gupta dynasty and who

< Legend says that anyone who circles this Gupta pillar near Delhi with their arms behind their backs will have a wish granted: But it's not so easy!

inherited many of the Guptas' cultural styles.

Physical evidence shows that prosperity went together with artistic excellence. Architects built fine temples, and sculptors carved images of the Buddha, the Hindu gods, and saints from another Indian religion, Jainism. Writers wrote great plays in Sanskrit that are still performed. Kalidasa, who likely worked at the court of Chandragupta, has been called India's Shakespeare.

Outposts of Buddhism

Over the years, the Guptas and other dynasties returned to the priest-led traditions of the Vedic period. In that way, they laid the basis for what we recognize as the Hindu religion today.

Buddhism survived in Nepal and on Sri Lanka. On the island, experts have been exploring a remarkable monument since 1982. On top of Sigiraya, a rock outcrop about 650 feet (200 m) high, stand the ruins of palaces, gardens, and a rock gallery painted with images of beautiful women. But the rock is so steep that after it was discovered in the early 1800s, it was 70 years before anyone climbed to the top.

The lion-shaped rock

Rock carvings show the history of the site on Sigiraya. In A.D. 477, a king named Kasyapa I started building a palace there, reached only by one dizzying set of stairs. Sigiraya means lion mountain. The rock got its name because from a distance it looks like a crouching lion.

Kasyapa was overthrown before his palace was even completed. The site became a Buddhist sanctuary for another 800 years, after which it was forgotten—as the Guptas and Buddhism in India would be for centuries.

◁ Gupta artists created a feeling of life and movement in statues such as this one of the Hindu god Vishnu.

Meet an Archaeologist

Kathleen Morrison is a professor of anthropology at the University of Chicago. She has worked on many excavations in India and elsewhere, specializing in studying plant remains.

What made you want to become an archaeologist?
I never thought about it until I tried it. I was interested in science, history, and anthropology, and one summer I worked on an excavation. I loved it—we were uncovering an ancient city, with streets, buildings, and even drains. It made history seem really alive, touching things that people had made and used and seeing things no one had seen for hundreds or even thousands of years.

When did you get interested in India?
I was in graduate school when I got a chance to work on a project in India. I knew I liked Indian food, so it seemed like a good idea. When I got there, in 1985, I found that India has an amazing and not very well-studied archaeological record. There is so much more to learn, which is very appealing, and the people are really wonderful. Fortunately, I still like Indian food.

What's the best part of your job?
Being an archaeologist at a university involves a lot of different things including teaching, lab work, writing, fieldwork, and service, which usually means going to meetings. I love fieldwork, especially when my colleagues, students, and I are working together. I also like spending time in the lab, where I study ancient plant remains. It's exciting when we find something unexpected.

What's the worst part of your job?
Archaeology can be pretty tedious. Sometimes we have to study thousands and thousands of things—pieces of pottery, pollen grains, or whatever—to begin to see a general pattern. This process can take years.

What are the most important qualities for an archaeologist?
A curiosity about and an interest in virtually everything! You have to be

able to work in teams and alone and to handle both numbers and words. Most jobs require a master's degree or Ph.D., so you have to go to graduate school. Persistence is also helpful, not only to get through all the training but also to keep working on a problem that might take years to resolve. Most archaeologists also like to be outside and to travel.

What's your favorite period in Indian history?
That's a hard one. Right now I am in the early years of a new project on the Iron Age and Early Historic periods in southern India, which started about 3,000 years ago (1000 BC) and lasted for around 1,500 years. At this time, the first cities and states appeared in the region, along with real differences in power and status between people. Southern Indians also began growing rice on a large scale. Rice takes a lot of water and a lot of work to grow, and it made a big impact on the environment. That all these things happened at around the same time is pretty amazing; we'd really like to know how and why.

What are the biggest challenges working in India?
It can be difficult to get permission to work from the government, and there is a lot of paperwork and long waits

Λ Kathleen Morrison's colleague Mark Lycett stands on top of the wall of an ancient reservoir during a survey in southern India.

every season. India is also very far from the U.S., so it is an expensive trip and one that is quite tiring.

What techniques have been most useful for your work?
One thing people may not always realize is that a lot of archaeological work deals with remains that are above ground. We spend a long time doing a survey of a large region, which involves walking back and forth in a very specific way, recording all archaeological sites. Our area is very hilly, so we had to climb a lot, wade through canals, stomp through muddy banana groves, and really work hard. We found

hundreds of sites, including villages, roads, temples, wells, reservoirs, iron-making sites, and many more. We needed good mapping and computer skills, knowledge of architecture, and of course a trained eye to see the remains of different time periods. No single person knows about everything, so archaeologists always work in teams. We have people who study animal bones, human remains, plant remains, metal working, soils and sediments, pottery, stone tools, and even beads. We send material to specialized labs to get radiocarbon dates and chemical analyses of sediments and other things.

The Living Past

Why does the past cause controversy today?

Archaeologists in South Asia face many challenges. For example, the division between India and Pakistan in 1947 left political and religious tensions in the region. Muslim dynasties ruled India from the 13th to the 19th centuries, but most Indians remained Hindus. Pakistan was created as a Muslim state, but more than 145 million Muslims still live in India. Some people in India want to show that Hindu culture is superior to that of Muslims. Some Muslims in Pakistan want to show the opposite.

< The Taj Mahal is still one of India's most popular historic sites—but it was built by a Muslim prince in an Islamic style.

^ At Kot Diji, a Mughal fort was built on top of the Harappan city. Such reuse of sites was common in ancient times, but today may cause controversy.

The past does not follow the political divisions of the present, however. The most famous ancient site in India is the Taj Mahal, which was built by a Muslim ruler in memory of his dead wife in the early 17th century. In Pakistan, on the other hand, the best-known sites are Harappa and Mohenjodaro. Both are thousands of years older than the Islamic religion.

Archaeology and nations

In the decades since independence, people in India and Pakistan—and also in Bangladesh and Sri Lanka— have seen archaeology as a way to strengthen the idea of their nation. They opened museums, for example, where people could see artifacts tracing the past. The ancient artifacts often make clear that the countries of the region shared a common past. They are sometimes placed near more recent displays about the achievement of independence. That encourages visitors to identify the past with their own nation.

Sometimes, competition between countries has spurred efforts to find out about the past. After Partition, for example, Harappa and Mohenjodaro lay in Pakistan. The ASI made it a priority to search for new Harappan sites, so that India could claim a closer link with Bronze Age cultures. As a result, the ASI made some spectacular discoveries, such as the city of Dholavira on India's west coast.

At other times, however, politics and religion have been damaging. In India, Hindu extremists have destroyed Islamic structures. In Pakistan, extremists have argued that experts should concentrate on Islamic sites, not older places such as Harappa.

A famous city

Not all archaeology in South Asia is so controversial. In 2002, experts from India's National Institute of Oceanography visited Mahabalipuram in Tamil Nadu to explore ruins in shallow water near the coast. There were stories that a city with seven temples once stood on the site. The city's beauty made the gods jealous. They sent a flood that destroyed six of the seven temples.

There are myths all over the world about ancient floods, and archaeologists do not always take them seriously. However, fishers led the team to an area of walls, broken pillars, and stone blocks on the seabed. Evidence from remains on land nearby suggested that the complex may have been built between 1,200 and 1,500 years ago. Not for the first time in Indian archaeology what seemed to be just a story did have a basis in fact.

A disaster reveals treasure

In December 2004, the coast around Mahabalipuram was battered by the Indian Ocean tsunami. The wave washed sand from beaches near the town and exposed more ruins. ASI archaeologists found two temples. One had been built in the ninth century A.D. on top of the ruins of a temple from the first century B.C. In the ground nearby, archaeologists found thick layers of seashells and other debris. They believe the layers were

∧ Local workers help clear debris from part of one of the temples exposed by the Indian Ocean tsunami in December 2004.

left by two earlier tsunamis, which destroyed the two temples.

Despite such discoveries, experts in the subcontinent still face problems. Relations between Pakistan and India are still tense. In India, meanwhile, some Hindu politicians are unhappy with the accepted version of history. They argue that Muslim rulers destroyed Indian culture, rather than adding to it. It seems that, until the political background changes, archaeology may continue to find itself in the middle of a tense fight.

The Years Ahead

There are lots of causes to be optimistic about archaeology in South Asia. Major projects at Harappa in Pakistan and at various sites run by the ASI in India are continuing to yield new information. In the half-century since India gained independence in 1947, generations of native experts have emerged to take the place of the British archaeologists who led most earlier work.

In both India and Pakistan, the governments are eager to make sure that ancient sites are well preserved. Some are still visited by pilgrims. Others are still used for worship. Many are included on the World Heritage Site list of the United Nations cultural department, UNESCO.

In the north, there is even good news from Afghanistan. The Taliban government destroyed some ancient statues—but many remain. And the Bactrian gold that was thought to have been lost turned up safely. After the U.S.-led invasion of 2001, experts opened six locked safes in the Kabul Museum—and found all 20,600 pieces of the treasure. Experts from the National Geographic Society helped to photograph and record the artifacts more carefully than anyone had been able to do in 1978, when the treasure was first discovered.

∧ **National Geographic photographer Kenneth Garrett prepares to photograph a piece of the Bactrian gold.**

Glossary

architect – a person who designs and builds buildings

artifact – any object changed by human activity

carbon – an element found in all living things; it can be used to date objects accurately

ceramics – objects made from clay

circa – about; used to indicate a date that is approximate (abbreviated as ca)

citadel – a fortress that defends a city

civil war – a war fought between groups of people from the same country

controversy – an argument between two opposite points of view

dynasty – a series of rulers that all come from the same family

excavation – an archaeological dig

extremist – a person who holds an extreme version of religious or political views

fossil – the remains of an ancient animal or plant that have been preserved in Earth's crust and turned to rock

foundation – the buried base that supports a building

hunter-gatherers – people who get food by hunting animals or gathering wild fruit and berries, rather than by farming

hymns – songs written to praise a god or gods

imperial – something associated with an empire or emperor

inscriptions – words that are carved or engraved into a hard material

kilns – ovens used to bake pottery to make it stronger

Muslim – a follower of the Islamic faith

pass – a valley that provides an easy pathway through a mountain range

ramparts – large banks of brick or earth that protect towns or other sites

relief – a carving with a raised surface

rituals – repeated practices that relate to specific ceremonies

sanctuary – the most holy part of a religious building

seal – an object used to stamp a pattern into soft clay or wax to identify the owner

semiprecious stones – colored stones that are shaped and polished to make jewelry or other objects

shards – broken pieces of pottery

silt – particles of soil carried in water that settle to form a kind of soil

stupa – a domed monument built by Buddhists and used to help meditation and prayer

subcontinent – a name usually given to the part of Asia that includes India, Pakistan, Nepal, Bhutan, Bangladesh, and Sri Lanka

theory – in science, the explanation that best explains all of the evidence

tsunami – a tidal wave caused by an earthquake beneath the seabed

urban – belonging to a city

ware – pottery such as plates and pots that have been made from clay and then baked in a kiln

zooarchaeology – the study of the past through the remains of animals

Bibliography

Books

Ancient India: Land of Mystery. Alexandria, VA: Time-Life Books, 1994.

Dehejia, Vidya. *Indian Art.* London: Phaidon Press, 1997.

Harle, J. C. *The Art and Architecture of the Indian Subcontinent.* New Haven: Yale University Press, 1994.

Keay, John. *A History of India.* New York: Grove Press, 2001.

Articles

Behl, Benoy K. "Striking New Images of Cave Paintings in India." NATIONAL GEOGRAPHIC (November 1993): Geographica.

"Brought to Light: New Dawn for a Night Garden at the Taj Mahal." NATIONAL GEOGRAPHIC (March 2001): Geographica.

Edwards, Mike. "Indus Civilization: Clues to an Ancient Puzzle." NATIONAL GEOGRAPHIC (June 2000): 108-131.

Further Reading

Aronovsky, Ilona, and Sujata Gopinath. *The Indus Valley* (Excavating the Past). Chicago: Heinemann, 2004.

Barr, Marilyn. *India: Exploring Ancient Civilizations.* Carthage, IL: Teaching and Learning Company, 2003.

Schomp, Virginia. *Ancient India* (People of the Ancient World). New York: Franklin Watts, 2005.

On the Web

The British Museum
http://www.ancientindia.co.uk/

History for Kids
http://www.historyforkids.org/learn/india/

Harappa Archaeological Research Project (HARP)
http://www.harappa.com/indus2/harpframe.html

UNESCO World Heritage List for India
http://whc.unesco.org/en/statesparties/in

UNESCO World Heritage List for Pakistan
http://whc.unesco.org/en/statesparties/pk

Index

About the Author

ANITA DALAL has an Indian father and a British mother and studied for her doctorate in London. She has traveled many times to India and visited many of its ancient sites. Today she is usually accompanied by her young son, but complains that it's exhausting trying to keep up with him.

About the Consultant

DR. MONICA L. SMITH is associate professor of anthropology at the University of California at Los Angeles. She is also director of the South Asian Laboratory at UCLA's Cotsen Institute of Archaeology, which houses reference material and facilities for studying the past of the Indian subcontinent. She is particularly interested in the growth of early cities, the archaeology of food, and the role of the ordinary person in prehistory.

< Statue of a man combining Indian and Greek influences, northern Pakistan, second–third century A.D.

934
DAL

One of the world's largest nonprofit
scientific and educational organizations, the
National Geographic Society was founded in
1888 "for the increase and diffusion of
geographic knowledge." Fulfilling this
mission, the Society educates and inspires millions
every day through its magazines, books, television
programs, videos, maps and atlases, research grants,
the National Geographic Bee, teacher workshops, and
innovative classroom materials. The Society is
supported through membership dues, charitable gifts,
and income from the sale of its educational products.
This support is vital to National Geographic's mission
to increase global understanding and promote
conservation of our planet through exploration,
research, and education.

For more information, please call 1-800-NGS-LINE
(647-5463) or write to the following address:

National Geographic Society
1145 17th Street N.W. *18.00*
Washington, D.C. 20036-4688
U.S.A.

Visit the Society's Web site:
www.nationalgeographic.com

Library of Congress Cataloging-in-Publication Data
available upon request
Hardcover ISBN: 978-1-4263-0070-7
Library ISBN: 978-1-4263-0071-4

Printed in Mexico

Series design by Jim Hiscott
The body text is set in Century Schoolbook
The display text is set in Helvetica Neue, Clarendon

National Geographic Society

John M. Fahey, Jr., *President and Chief Executive
Officer;* Gilbert M. Grosvenor, *Chairman of the Board;*
Nina D. Hoffman, *Executive Vice President, President of
Book Publishing Group*

Staff for This Book

Nancy Laties Feresten, *Vice President, Editor-in-Chief
of Children's Books*
Virginia Ann Koeth, *Project Editor*
Bea Jackson, *Director of Design and Illustration*
David M. Seager, *Art Director*
Lori Epstein, National Geographic Image Sales,
Illustrations Editors
Jean Cantu, *Illustrations Specialist*
Carl Mehler, *Director of Maps*
Priyanka Lamichhane, *Assistant Editor*

R. Gary Colbert, *Production Director*
Lewis R. Bassford, *Production Manager*
Maryclare Tracy, Nicole Elliott *Manufacturing
Managers*

For the Brown Reference Group, plc
Tim Cooke, *Managing Editor*
Alan Gooch, *Book Designer*

Photo Credits
Front: © Dagli Orti/Musée Guimet Paris/The Art
Archive
Back: © Jean-Louis Nou/AKG Images
Spine: © Heather Lewis/Shutterstock
Icon: © Apury Shah/Shutterstock

NGIC = National Geographic Image Collection
1, © Jean-Louis Nou/AKG Images; 2-3, © George F.
Mobley/NGIC; 4, © Charles & Josette Lenars/Corbis; 6,
© Heather Lewis/Shutterstock; 8, © Monica L. Smith;
10, © Angelo Hornak/Corbis; 10-11, © Angelo Hornak/
Corbis; 11, © Barney Burstein/Corbis;12-13, © Lindsay
Hebberd/Corbis; 14, © Lindsay Hebberd/Corbis; 15 top,
© Kazuyoshi Nomachi/Corbis; 15 bottom, © James P
Blair/NGIC; 16, © Adam Woolfitt/Corbis; 17, © Jenny
Pate/Eye Ubiqitous/Hutchison; 18-19, © Randy Olson/
NGIC; 20, © James P Blair/NGIC; 21, © James P Blair/
NGIC; 22, © Randy Olson/NGIC; 23 top, © Randy
Olson/NGIC; 23 right, © Randy Olson/NGIC; 24, ©
Randy Olson/NGIC; 25, © Harry Bliss/NGS; 26, ©
James P Blair/NGIC; 27, © James P Blair/NGIC; 28-29,
© Charles & Josette Lenars/Corbis; 30, © Maggie
Steber/NGIC; 31, © Jean-Luis Nou/AKG Images; 32, ©
Randy Olson/NGIC; 33, © Angelo Hornak/Corbis; 34-
35, © Nevada Wier/Corbis; 36 top, © Suzanne Held/
AKG Images; 36 bottom, © Jenny Pate/Eye Ubiquitous
& Hutchison; 37 © Bennett Dean/Eye Ubiqutous &
Hutchison; 38, © Theresa McCullough Collection,
London/Werner Forman Archive; 39, © Jon Burbank/
Eye Ubiquitous & Hutchison; 40-41, © Burstein
Collection/Corbis; 42 top, © Patricio Goycoolea/Eye
Ubiquitous & Hutchison; 42 bottom, © Jean-Louis Nou/
AKG Images; 43 © David Flemming/Eye Ubiquitous &
Hutchison; 44, © Kenneth Garrett/ NGIC; 45 top, ©
Kenneth Garrett/NGIC; 45 bottom, Viktor Ivanovich
Sarianidi/NGIC; 46-47, © James P Blair/NGIC; 48, ©
James P Blair/NGIC; 49, © James P Blair/NGIC; 50, ©
James L Stanfield/NGIC; 51, © James P Blair/NGIC;
52, © Kathleen Morrison; 53, © Kathleen Morrison ;54-
55, © Kamel Kishore/Reuters/Corbis, 56, © Randy
Olson/NGIC; 57, © Pallava Bagla/Corbis; 58, ©
Kenneth Garrett/NGIC; 63, © Theresa McCullough
Collection, London/Werner Forman Archive

Front cover: 11th-12th century sculpture of Vishnu
from Madhya Pradesh.
Page 1 and back cover: This sculpture from a temple
at Khajuraho shows a prince killing a lion.
Pages 2–3: Elephants are taken to drink from a river
at dusk.